WHAT DOES BACH PROVE?

Kevin Don Levellie

Revised Edition

Contact Information:

Kevin Don Levellie

17475 E 390th Road, Paris Il 61944

217-463-8770 or 217-712-1287

KDLevellie@gmail.com

On Facebook as Kevin Levellie

Blog at http://levellies.blogspot.com;

More books available at www.lulu.com

ISBN #: 978-1-329-35186-8

Introduction

I cannot imagine living in a world without the music of Bach. I wonder what they could have listened to before he came. Oh, I know there were many fine musicians and composers who predate him. To take one example, Buxtehude must have been something pretty special for Bach to have walked over 250 miles to hear him play and spend a quarter of a year absorbing his music. I have a set of Buxtehude's complete organ music, so I've heard anything Bach could have heard, albeit I didn't hear Buxtehude playing it. It's pretty good, but it's not Bach. I think Bach went well beyond him, but still, there was something there. But... To imagine a world in which I couldn't listen to Bach's music would seem bizarrely strange.

One day in the fall of 2014 I began to think about what this music meant. I wasn't trying for any particular number of points, but almost as fast as it took to pen them down, I wrote ten things on the back of an old church bulletin and stopped. They seemed to form a complete list. I kept thinking about them and decided I wanted to explore them. Books don't always present what the author already knows. The writing often brings out into the open what is thought, but which has been previously unexpressed in concrete terms.

Bach lived from 31 March 1685 to 28 July 1750. What concerned him concerns me. But why should someone who lived so long ago concern me? He died centuries before I was born. He didn't live in my country and wasn't a part of my culture. He did nothing political or scientific which shaped or changed the course of history, yet this one man, almost singlehandedly, without possibly even realizing that he was doing it, set the course for Western music.

Music is of utmost importance. Someone once said that he didn't care who wrote his country's laws as long as he could write her songs. We don't really know the fine points of politics in the eras of "Yankee Doodle Dandy" or "Dixie", but we still know those songs in our souls and whatever their composers and singers stood for, they stand for.

Every musician knows that Bach was important, but I have, strictly from hearing his compositions without going into any history or musicological parsing of his works, explored why he continues to be important.

This book took a lot longer than I had expected it to take. I kept discovering something more I wanted to say or add or clarify about Bach's music. There are more paths to follow than can be imagined beforehand.

My book is subjective. It's not about Bach in a historic setting, nor is it a musicological analysis of his music. It's about Bach in my life and musical schematic.

There were no written sources consulted for my analyses. They came from only listening to the music, and, even though I had heard these pieces over and over, I listened to them again with an appraising ear to dig deeper and mine out what Bach proves in them.

Most of what I know historically about Bach comes from album liner notes, articles in the "BBC Music Magazine", and one book, which I would recommend, The Bach Reader, edited by Hans T. David and Arthur Mendel.

I'm not interested in psychoanalyzing the man and his influences as has been done in so many modern biographies, even those of fictional characters, but in continuing my personal acquaintance with Bach's music.

I explored the concept of a personal music schematic and briefly looked at Bach's place in mine in You Have To Love It The Value Of Classical Music. This present book, too, is about experiencing music as an end-user.

Everyone has to listen for himself. No one can do your listening for you. I do not intend that you hear what I hear or understand as I understand, but that by reading about what I think as a result of Bach's music, you'll begin to find something for yourself, if not in Bach, then in a composer of your own schematic. There are values waiting to be discovered and absorbed.

Since I will be using the term "schematic" throughout this book, I would like to take a moment to clarify what I mean by it. I originally heard of the concept of having a musical schematic from an article in the BBC Music Magazine back in the 1990s. I didn't use the definition of the article, but developed my own take on it. This is how I put it in <u>You Have To Love It</u>:

> "I have a schematic inside myself of the culture of my heart. It includes the music which is a part of me. It is a construct containing the entire body of my musical preferences placed on a sort of grid of genres, types and styles. It is a pattern which puts everything in relationship to myself and what I like."

When I speak of a schematic, I am referring too all the music which I am at home with. This is a matter of heart. Bach has an especially large spot on my grid.

I was going to call this book "What <u>Did</u> Bach Prove?" Then, I realized that the tense was wrong. It's not what he proved in the past, but what he is continuing to prove in the present that concerns us. He proves these to those who play or listen to his music. I cannot say of my own knowledge whether he set out to prove what I found, but in his music he proved more than the notes did.

Bach is not as accessible to many modern listeners as some of the later classical and romantic era composers are, but he is worth the time and energy it takes to get to know him. Even if a person was so modernized that he had never heard Bach's music, he would know it nonetheless, for Bach is there in those who followed him. He is the greatest of all. Few would deny him that place, but even those who have another candidate for greatest would not dismiss Bach as being nothing. Great composers have studied him in order to learn the basics. Then, they used him as a springboard to express themselves. I appreciate him as a musician of my soul. He not only wrote the greatest music, but established more over a broader spectrum of the human spirit and intellect than any other individual composer ever did.

I would like to share one more thing before plunging in, even though it should be fairly obvious from the title of the first chapter. I am writing from the context of my Christian faith just as Bach wrote from the context of his faith throughout his life. There will be mentions of faith and scripture and Jesus and their connection with the music and with life throughout. That's why the book is more front heavy. These are the first things, and they are the strongest things. They are woven into my love and understanding of this music, and, mutually, the music enhances them. There's no way I could look at it without them.

1 The Story Of Jesus Is Important

Bach tells the story of Jesus with beauty and art and fire. That's how the story should be told, because that's the kind of story it is.

The first draft of every chapter was written while some of the music under discussion was being played. I didn't depend on memories of the past or impressions or feelings about the music, but on the experience of the music itself in the present. It is, of course, the feelings which bring me back, but the music itself is what demands the repeated listenings.

My piano teacher often referred to Bach, Beethoven and Brahms as the three B's. I don't know that I ever played any of his music when I was taking piano lessons other than perhaps some very simplified works in the graded piano material we went through. I remember that we played a version of "Komm Susser Tod" in our high school orchestra, but it didn't seem to make any lasting impression on me. Bach was a big name then, but it wasn't until much later that I took up an acquaintance with him as a person.

The real beginning of my relationship starts with the St. Matthew Passion which is why I begin this book with it. That was when Bach first got a handle on me.

The term, "Passion", despite modern connotations of the word, does not mean an overwhelming emotional feeling of desire for someone or something, but a total expenditure of the person in agony undertaken for a specific purpose. Rather than a term of euphoria, it is one of struggle. I don't like to see the word used lightly as it sometimes come to be used to describe an intense interest in or commitment to something. This word should be kept in reserve for use with regard to the absolutely extraordinary act rather than the astonished feeling.

Jesus lived 33 years, but the event we label the Passion didn't even take up 33 hours of his life. We normally start our accounting with the agony in the garden and complete it with the death on the cross. It is what Jesus underwent in entire time period which did not encompass a full day. It may not have been much more than 15 hours, a little less than the time we normally spend awake in an average day, but it included betrayal, denial, six successive intensive interrogations, a severe beating, humiliation in private and public, a cruel and horrific six hour death during which he underwent more misunderstanding and ridicule by those who saw Him during His time on the cross as well as a realization that He still had unfinished business to take care of with regard to family while keeping Himself aware and unclouded by any amelioration of the pain until the final release from the body of death. That is more than I would want to deal with in an entire lifetime.

A Passion is something that can be gone through only once. It consumes whoever goes through it. Jesus had nothing more physically to contribute to us once this was finished. What He set out to do was accomplished. It needed nothing more in the physical realm. This is the story Bach found significant and important, and it is the story which he poured his best music into.

Back to my first encounter with a Bach Passion. I got a four lp set of the St. Matthew Passion for $5.00 in a bargain bin at a music store in San Jose when I was a freshman at San Jose Bible College. I don't remember the names of the singers, orchestra or conductor, but this was the second time I had bought a recording in which the music so dominated the recording as to make it almost more than a recording. The first had been a recording of Beethoven's 9th symphony I had acquired when I was in high school played by the Boston Symphony Orchestra under Charles Munch.

The St. Matthew was the longest classical piece I had ever heard. For sheer mass in terms of length, it surpassed Beethoven's 9th and even edged out Handel's Messiah. (About this same time period I acquired my first recording of that work as well.) As I didn't have a record player of my own at the time, I had to listen to my records through headphones on a player at the Bible College library. I think it took three sessions to listen to the whole thing.

I was captivated by the music from the very beginning of my first listen through. Some works need to be heard to the end before their importance can be understood or else they need to be experienced several times over a long period to absorb them into my personal music schematic, but the opening bars declared the importance and power of this work. It was not just a work of strength, but one which became at home in my heart.

It's not surprising that this piece affected me so much because it was the work which Mendelssohn used to inaugurate a Bach revival. Mendelssohn knew what he was doing. His choice was no fluke. This work had been neglected, yet it was and is perhaps the single most important work of Bach's. Bringing it to the public's attention changed everything, and today things continue to be changed from what they were before Mendelssohn's performance.

I wonder what would have become of Bach if Mendelssohn had not done this? Would he have been another composer like Vivaldi who languished in obscurity for centuries before finally being re-discovered? Would anyone have ever "found" him? What would have happened in the meantime? Would we have taken someone else to our hearts? Thank God the what-ifs are not our reality.

I had no idea what I was going to hear the first time through. Other than understanding the length of the Passion which I assumed was going to be good value for $5.00, I didn't know how it would play out. Being from the same era, it might have been along the lines of "The Messiah", but it was the story of Jesus taken in a completely different direction. Rather than a series of well known choruses and solos, we have a piece in which all is integrated into a whole. Handel's work has an overwhelming brilliance and greatness. Bach's has depth and breadth. The gospels fit into music in a way I had never heard before.

There continues to be power in the orchestra's commencement of the story. From the very first time I heard the work, I was struck with the utter seriousness of the approach. Here was something which Bach fully intended to work out to it's full end. This was not a flighty throw-away potboiler. Here was something which we were to pay attention to in a way that we were to pay attention to nothing else which came along.

The orchestra doesn't play alone long until the choir comes in. Instantly, we are moved beyond the statement of the instruments. We are catapulted into the words. I don't know German, and, even in English I can't always follow the words in such pieces without intense concentration, but the music speaks to me powerfully. In some ways, not knowing the language leaves me free to listen with my heart rather than my head. The voice gives expression to more than the words. It embodies the entire emotional and spiritual force of the account.

The dialogue between the chorus and the individual voices is just like the story in the gospel. We have both the crowds and the narrations, and then we have the individual speakers. It takes all of them to tell the story. This is not something told by a clever raconteur who does it all himself. This requires Jesus at the center, but also all the forces and individuals around Him in order for the full story to come out.

One thing I have noticed over the years in continually listening to this piece is that, despite the length of it, it never lags or becomes too long. I'm never ready for it to be over. It is a story which is told in the time necessary to complete it. You can't hurry it to a conclusion. If anything, it keeps the conclusion at bay until everything is complete. This is a story of absolute completion.

Facts alone don't make a story. Stories require a certain amount of exposition in order to be interesting. If we say, "A man was born, lived and died," what interest is there? It may be a true story, but even if we give the name, and it happens to be a well known name, there is no significance to it as a story. It is a succession of facts in narrative and sequential relationship along with events and personal actions and the consequences of those actions to both the individual spoken of and those around him which make it a story. Also, a story never rambles on meaninglessly, but it has a point and a conclusion. It arrives somewhere.

Sometimes we are told stories which are unsatisfactory. This is usually because they don't provide a conclusion which fits the preceding narrative or because there was too much or too little information given before the end to make it seem like a conclusion. The good story gives a perfect balance of all the events so that it can be understood. The story of Jesus in the gospels does this. Bach knew it and demonstrated it in his construction of this work. Unlike his more cerebral works, such as the Well-Tempered Clavier or The Art Of The Fugue, we know here that we have been told something, and it was something important enough that Bach took longer to tell it than he did on anything else he wrote.

Length of time is not always an indication of importance. One contemporary composer has written a piece which is now being performed which is so long that no one alive today will be alive when the performance of the piece is completed. There have been many musical pieces, books and films which go on for hours and leave the consumer senseless, wondering what he has experienced at the end. Not the St. Matthew. It could have gone on another hour or two, and I would have never tired of it.

This is an experience which needs to be taken to the end. Some pieces you can hear a little bit of and then be done. Many people find Ravel's "Bolero" a bore or a waste of time with it's incessant incremental repetition, seemingly going nowhere until the hurried resolution in the last moment which doesn't even give you time to enjoy it. I do listen to it from time to time if it happens to be on a recording with other music I'm wanting to hear, but I don't usually pick out a recording for the purpose of hearing the "Bolero". Ravel had something in particular in mind that he was trying to prove by that composition, but it doesn't get to the heart like the music of Bach does.

All the time we are in the St. Matthew we know we are going somewhere. I'm never in a hurry to get to the end. This is the kind of piece that a person could almost begin listening to again as soon as the final note sounded, and he wouldn't be over-listening to it.

Interestingly, as this gets closer to the end, it slows down and gets less intense. The anger of man has exhausted itself, and now we are thinking about the triumph of God. It is a battle story, but not one which turns on the brilliant activity of the hero commander, but one which only works because, as in the old

Greek tragedies, the hero is crushed. Jesus is not crushed because of some fault within Himself, but because of the faults within all of us.

Then, we come to the last chorus. We can feel the intensity in the musicians, not a wild dithyrambic movement, but rather a settled arrival at the completion of the work.

Sometimes when something is completed in life, the ending of it creeps up on us unawares. We're waiting for more, but getting nothing more, we finally have to conclude that it has concluded. There are no fireworks and there doesn't seem to be a sense of release. We have been so long at the work that we don't know where to go with it or past it. To no longer do it doesn't seem "right", but we don't know what should come next. Bach's work is different.

At the end of the Passion we arrive at rest. It comes down, just as Jesus came down from the cross. He goes to the tomb, not in defeat, but in anticipation of what is to come next. There is confidence in the final notes and even in the silence which follows them. We are not dissatisfied.

Satisfaction is one of the greatest assessments that can be made of any work. It completely meets and fills us. This is not only true of Bach's composition, but, more importantly, of Jesus' sacrifice for us.

Jesus actually completed this task and released it and went away from it. On this day, he left it through the door of death, but He would come back to proclaim the reality of what He had done by demonstrating His power over death and all of the physical world by walking through walls and yet demonstrate He was still one of us by eating some fish. This part of the story is beyond the scope of Bach's work, but we can certainly expect it by the way Bach closed this work out. He never intended for it to be the end.

I got my first recording of the St. John Passion in the 1990s. Since then, I have acquired two different cd sets of both Passions and have heard them through streaming on the internet from the BBC radio network, but I had never heard the piece or even a portion of it on the radio or in any other media before buying it. I came to it fresh as I had come to the St. Matthew so many years earlier.

I was kind of disappointed in the St. John the first time I heard it. It had a strange feel. I was expecting "more of the same". I had owned my St. Matthew for over 20 years and was very familiar with it. This was a case where I had to do some schematic expanding, although at the time I didn't know that that was what I was doing.

The St. John was not a carbon copy of the St. Matthew. It was much heavier and even more strident. It was as if we had picked up the intensity and were even more serious than we had been before.

I would have to say that I still prefer the St. Matthew to the St. John, but it could be that I'm just a little bit uncomfortable with the St. John music. I don't know that I ever analyzed it that way before I sat down to listen to these two pieces back to back as I began to write this chapter. Things aren't as easy from John as they were from Matthew. Matthew as a writer concentrated more on the events in his gospel. John often dug beneath the surface to comment on the significance of the events. His whole book starts out in that light. It paints a cosmic picture which we are responsible to engage with. Responsibility is not always comfortable.

There is definitely an urgency to the beginning of the St. John music. It's as if we are made aware that we don't have all the time in the world to do something about this. Even the recitatives seem more pointed. There is a definite edge to the music, more than there is with the normal baroque work of the era.

What Jesus did was not merely a dramatic story. It was the solution to the problem of the world. When I was a kid they used to have some math text books which would give answers to half the problems in the back of the book. The teachers, of course, knew all about this, so they assigned the questions which did not have printed answers in the text. We were to use the answers provided to help us understand the nature of the problems and their solutions so we could arrive at the answers where they were not provided. When it came to math I didn't do a very good job of that. I just couldn't seem to make the logical connections to find the principles by which the answers to the other problems could be achieved. I stick to the four math functions which I do understand and leave algebra, geometry and everything beyond them to others. I don't take responsibility for those fields.

The story of Jesus demands an answer. It demands belief. I have to take responsibility in the face of it. John, particularly, is the gospel writer aiming at belief. It's no wonder Bach would write more challenging music here. We have moved from reporting an event to requiring attendance at it and to it.

Jesus knows we can't come to logical conclusions about anything on our own, so He provides the answer, not just to some of the problems, but to all of the problems. His intention is that we should make them our own answers. This isn't cheating; it is agreement. Some professors and teachers make no bones about the fact that they may not have it right, but that you had better put it how they put it on the final in order to get a good grade.

God has it right, so when we agree with Him we are agreeing with what is right. God is incredibly interested in having us concur with Him. If He had not been, He would not have sent Jesus. He would have just dealt with sin and us as He saw fit and been done with it.

What are the problems we deal with?

❖ Selfishness

❖ Pride

❖ Guilt

❖ Sorrow from guilt

❖ A limited physical life

❖ Lack of direct access to God

These are hardly all of them, but they give an idea. People will often live in denial as to some or all of these, but they still have to cope with them. Notice it doesn't say anything in the list I gave about money or getting a job or success, although Jesus, by providing access to the Father through prayer, does give the answer to such things.

The Passion story is a suffering story. Suffering is not a value in itself. It has to be connected with something objective in order to do anyone any good. It has to produce something. It is never an end, but always a way through to something else.

We usually look away from the sufferings of others. I don't know whether suffering makes us uncomfortable thinking that maybe we should or will have some suffering of our own some day or whether we just feel it's impolite to stare.

When Jesus died it was in the full sight of the world. His execution did not take place behind prison walls in a small room with only a requisite number of legal witnesses. Anyone there in Jerusalem that day could have seen it if they could have gotten there.

There is something unsettling about shame displayed in public. We want to cover it up. We want to write it off as something else. We want to minimize it. Jesus did no minimizing at all. If anything, He maximized the human experience by coming in a well-publicized birth (angels and stars didn't attend anyone else's birth), revealing Himself through signs and wonders, and finally dying a naked, emotion wrenching death.

The nakedness of Jesus is not merely bad taste. It is a full demonstration that it is a male which is dying for the sins of the world. Jesus fulfilled everything required of a sacrifice in the Old Testament. Now, I don't think that element is in either of Bach's Passions, but the music makes me think of the exposure of Jesus. There is nothing mystical or hidden here. It is seen by God and the world that God has made provision for sin on the cross.

There seems to be more prominence to female soloists in the St. John than in the St. Matthew. I'm not sure if that is actually so on a quantifiable basis, but I am struck with the impression that the female presence seems more forward as I am listening to it now.

Bach deems this a story not just to be told by men, but by men and women. It is a story which deserves and calls for comment. God Himself commented on Jesus at the baptism and transfiguration. By His silence in the darkness at the crucifixion He silently said, "No comment," but then in the resurrection He commented as loudly as He could.

Even we, at this late date, are expected to put in our two cents' worth about Jesus. We should be singing our own accompaniment to what Jesus has done, not necessarily always with our lips, but certainly with our lives. Bach knew that, and he did it with his music. If anything, in the past several years, rather than growing less, the number of recordings and performances of this work seems to have increased. We have not finished with it.

The St. John seems to arrive at its end more quietly than the St. Matthew did. The St. Matthew leaves us in triumph; the St. John in peace. It's as if all cause for turmoil is at an end. We know that the early church would face severe persecution in the opposition from the world to follow as recorded in the book of Acts, but the main work of the world of all time has been finished. The world may furiously rage, but we are not moved by it for we are anchored to God through the cross of Christ.

Altogether, according to his obituary, Bach wrote five passions, but only these two have come down to us undisputedly. I have heard the choruses without any recitatives of a re-constructed St. Mark which I understand are mostly recycled music. I have a recording of an "apocryphal" (that word applies to Bach's composership, not to the author of the gospel) St. Luke one. There is value in even unattested music in an of itself. I have appreciated this work and will continue to listen to it, but I don't think it belongs in the discussion here other than to say that if someone else did write this music and they appended Bach's name to it to try to get it a larger circulation, it shows that they valued the story of Jesus, too.

Composers have always written about what is important to them or to their listeners. Oh, I know there are composers who have written works about Jesus or on Biblical themes who didn't believe or who were even actively antagonistic to Christ and the gospel system, but they did so for their listeners or to receive payment for a commission. Their lack of belief left them free to write anything that anyone wanted to hear.

I do not believe that Bach would have written godless music had there been pagan or atheistic listeners who wanted to hear something to fit their ideological likings. I have written hundreds of songs, but I would never accept a commission, even for a lot of money, to write a song in praise of another "god". Even if I thought it was just going to be regarded as an "art" song or one for the sake of "music", I would not do it. I believe that Bach only wrote about what really mattered to him in these passions. This was not someone else's idea of what was important. It was **his** idea.

Bach manages to make this story special. Though it has become almost commonplace to the most casual churchgoer through the annual Good Friday repetition, it is even more extraordinary than we treat it in our services. It is a story which demands exceptional handling. It is not a tale to be known or told, but one to be experienced. In the passions we do exactly that. They are almost a "You Are There" approach in the musical world with exposure to dialogue and then what amounted to Baroque news commentary.

Now, if you are an atheist and don't believe in Jesus, you might well say that Bach proves nothing here. I don't think that anyone who knows the life and mentality of Bach could say that, though. This is what he set out to express. Even though sometimes musical events are categorized differently, this is one which can only be categorized as a profession of belief. Bach may not prove the facts of the story through some kind of historical logical demonstration, but he proves the power and significance of the story by his handling of it. He proves the importance of the story by making it important.

I believe that it would not have mattered to Bach if every person on the face of the earth rejected the story. He would have kept writing about it because he held to it firmly and shared it with us on that basis.

In <u>The Bach Reader</u> there is information given as to the rigorous requirements of singers who would be a part of Bach's Thomaskirche Choir. I don't know where and with what choirs the Passions were sung originally, but I believe Bach would have used the best singers and musicians he would have had at his disposal. Now, I know that the worst can sing the story of Jesus as well, for He is pleased with the singing of all. No one is excluded from it's telling, but something which is worthy of the best is shown to be worthy of anyone, and that's what Bach showed. He made the music of the story of Jesus compelling and challenging and worth doing and re-doing as it has been done through the centuries.

The Passions tell us that the story of Jesus is important and that the story of the cross is the heart of the story of Jesus. It is what is different about this story from any other story. Other men have willingly died, but their deaths were not prophesied in detail centuries ahead of the event. Some have died undeservedly, but it came to nothing. When all the others died, it was the end of their story. When Jesus died, it was the crossroad of history and humanity. From that time on man was able to change his destiny from hell to heaven.

This music, while it does not take us on to the resurrection, does not "celebrate" the death, but proclaims it for what it is - our release from death and our ability to enter into the presence of God.

Bach proves that it is not our talents which make the story, but the story which makes us and makes use of whatever talents we have.

With no instrumental introduction at all, the B minor mass, the greatest mass ever written, starts calling on the Lord. Bach knows that this matter of bringing ourselves into the Lord's presence is so urgent that nothing should get in its way. We can't prepare for it; we just have to do it. Yet, how often do we have to work our way up to enthusiasms in our church services with preludes and rousing introductions.

Bach is giving us an example as to what **we** can do in and through and for the church. It's not that the church is worth something as an independent organization. We are the church. It is not something outside ourselves, but we are a body which Jesus died for and which He is now working for. We are significant. We are not worms of nothingness, but those being sanctified and fitted for heaven. What we do for one another and for the kingdom as a whole is worth it.

I wondered how much this music of Bach's is used in the average Lutheran church today, so I asked the local Lutheran pastor for his perspective on Bach's usage. He said that there were only six hymn settings by Bach in the hymnal they were using, but that Lutherans certainly have a sense of the music of Bach. As to frequency of use, his reply was, "Let's just say Mr. Bach is used regularly. Also nary a Lutheran wedding goes by without some of Mr. Bach's music. Most popular would be 'Jesus Joy of Man's desiring' for the Bride's processional." They are likely to use pieces that go with the lectionary setting for the year as those events come up, too. He also commented that, "Lutherans in general are aware of Mr. Bach as one of their 'own'."

We don't have much to do with Bach in our congregational singing. I've never been in a church which did. We only have one piece by him in our hymnal, and that is his arrangement of the hymn tune written for "O Sacred Head Now Wounded" by Hans Leo Hassler. I'm not sure that most people in my brotherhood would even recognize that song. Still, it's not our usage which proves what Bach proves. The amount of music he wrote for the church and the church year is a tremendous testimony of their importance.

I don't think we have anyone in any church today who is writing his own music for his own choir at his own church as prodigiously as Bach did. I write songs for Vacation Bible School every year, but writing a cantata once a week would be a definitely daunting task, especially as I don't know orchestration. I did write an a capella mass once, not because I'm a Catholic, but because I had read an issue of the "BBC Music Magazine" about sacred choral music, and I decided that I wanted to do something that Bach and Haydn had done, especially as I didn't think I knew enough about the various instruments and their scoring to be able to write symphonies or large scale choral works. That mass has yet to be performed, but one day I'd like to hear it. Even if I never do, though, the writing of the music was the gift Jesus has already received.

Bach didn't have long to wait to know about whether his work was well or not. I don't imagine he was writing that far ahead of performance dates. We hear these works in as a body of work all at once now, but I wonder if the people who originally heard them realized the lasting significance of what they were hearing or if they just thought, "Well, that was the music for this Sunday."

I don't think anyone who hears the B minor could think that. I read years ago that this kind of music was no longer being used in churches in worship services, but exclusively in the concert hall. I imagine that is true since it's beyond the average church musician in America, but even in the concert hall, it reflects back on the church. This is "our" music, not the world's. If the world wants to use it, we rejoice, but it will never be their music. It will always be Jesus'.

There is power in the B minor. It never sits still. It has a driving force. On that level, I would say that it could stand up against the later masses by Haydn, Mozart, Beethoven and Schubert. It excels them in stamina and durability. I probably listen to it more than all of the masses of those composers combined.

Too often, we hurry through our church music or wish that it wasn't taking so long or that there weren't so many verses.

There is life here in Bach which holds the attention. The mark of such a piece is the desire that it continue on indefinitely. This, of course, will be true of the music of heaven. It will go on and on without being in the least boring or monotonous. Bach knew that the church needed to learn that such music existed now so that she would be able to enter into it heaven. Having said that, though, I must point out that the work comes to a definite pointed conclusion. We know we're done, but it was so great that we don't quite know where to go from here. It's as if the world stopped when the piece stopped, and only we are going on. I wonder what the effect of a live performance would be?

Strange to say, but even people who class themselves as non-religious and who would very openly tell you that they do not care at all for Jesus Christ will devote their attention to the B minor mass. Why would they do that, if they didn't believe it? There is a power of the personality of Bach in the music which draws the listener to it. If Bach had a concern at all in this regard, it would be that people would be drawn to Jesus through what they heard.

The music of Bach was never a dead end. It was never intended for itself. It was always a threshold to greater things. No matter what the secular forces try to do with it, you cannot isolate the music of Bach away from Jesus. His is the name stamped all over it.

I first heard the B minor a couple of years after my initiation into the St. Matthew Passion. It was another bargain bin college lp purchase. Sadly, the days of the bargain bin seem to be over with regard to classical music; for the beginner, it was a great help to finding things he wouldn't be able to afford or might not have wanted to take a chance on. That lp has long since gone. It was used up almost as much as the St. Matthew. It was first replaced on cd by the Robert Shaw recording from the 1950s. Since then, I've added one by Harry Christophers and the Sixteen. It is a work which has always held my attention.

I particularly enjoy the Shaw recording despite its age. According to the liner notes, they recorded this after they had been on the road all summer long performing it. From personal experience, I know that performance in front of audiences sharpens a group more than any amount of practice behind closed doors. There is a wealth of intensity and emotion to this recording which gives proof to that. I believe it is still in the catalogue. If you can only get one, get this one.

Besides the mass in B minor, Bach wrote four shorter masses. They are not as striking, but they should probably have a little more play than they get. They certainly belong in the same league as the cantatas, and it is to the cantatas, however, that we are most indebted to Bach for penetration of the church by his music.

There are about 200 sacred cantatas in the Bach oeuvre. There are many complete recordings available. I have two plus individual recordings of some. If I had the money there are two more complete sets I'd like to get. This is music which is worth hearing over and over from as many vantage points as you can hear them from. The recording I probably value the most is a individual budget label recording of Cantatas 44, 78, 112. These are not driving performances, but they are by the Thomanerchor of Leipzig. This is the group Bach directed for many years. Most of the cantatas probably were premiered by this group. It's probably only in my head, but I can feel a connection there that I don't feel with other recordings.

The cantatas are so many that I don't have a handle on all of them and their various distinctions, but I can play a recording of any one and be on a spiritual plane. Probably the most distinctive is BWV 80 which is the one connected with Reformation Day since it uses Luther's famous tune in the midst of the work.

The cantatas balance orchestral forces, choral forces and soloists. They give a sense of unity, completeness and accomplishment. That's how the church operates. There are variously gifted individuals, some of which cooperate with other individuals in certain ministries and others who perform solo, but they all operate as the one church of Jesus Christ. And, like the cantatas, they all have something to say.

Bach has a few Oratorios, although none of them are on the scale of Handel's except the Christmas Oratorio which is technically the stringing together of six cantatas each designated for a particular day in the season. It is, like the Passions, one of the major works connected with the church year, and Christmas season would seem very strange without at least one listen to this work. The opening notes instantly carry me straight to the Christmas story.

While we are at Christmas, we must not overlook the Magnificat. I have heard many Magnificats by many composers; they continue to be written even into contemporary times. The scriptural text is a great one. It has more than enough material to work with. Bach's music is commensurate with the text in its greatness and power.

The other two Bach oratorios I usually listen to during the year are the Easter and Ascension ones. Even after several years of listening, though, they don't have the recognizable moments or the pull that the Passions and the B minor mass have. That only proves that even though a work cannot be at the top, it can still be worth an investment of time and effort to listen.

The Brilliant Classics set includes Bach's chorales. These are short, mostly in the minute and a half to three minute range. Some of them appear to be excerpts from larger works and others are variations on previous chorales, probably arranged for specific occasions. These are probably the kinds of things which are still being used in some worship services. I am so used to the large scale Bach, that it's hard to get excited about these. There's just not enough to them. They're over before I've barely started. But, they speak the language of God, and I can tell it's there when I hear them.

The music for the church is designed to teach and to aid in bringing home the message of the liturgical year to the listener. While I'm not a high church person, it is good to tie such music into our entire year. I can see the value of that. Our worship should be connected with the highest arts available.

Now, nothing that Bach did was bad, but this was where he did his best. Taking the Passions and organ works composed for church use into account as well, these are the highest points of Bach's work. He did his best work for his fellow Christians and all of his work for his Lord.

3 There Is Infinite Variety

Nothing begins more simply. It doesn't appear to be in a hurry, no matter who I've heard playing it. Yet, it is the heart and soul of Bach's instrumental music. I don't know that I'll ever have the skill to play it, but it's enough to be able to listen. If this was all we had, we would know that Bach was a real contender, not just a wannabe.

It's unfair to pick out a single work as though we are judging the composer in his entirety on the basis of it, yet when we speak of the Goldberg Variations, that's about the case. They are in a class by themselves. They have created careers and shaped everything that followed them. They never pale in the playing or the listening. Life is variety. These variations prove that for they are alive.

There is nothing else like the Goldbergs in either Bach's corpus or in the entirety of the classical repertoire. When I began to seriously collect classical music records, I found out that Beethoven did a composition called the Diabelli Variations, so I got a recording of it, expecting that the Goldberg experience would be taken up several notches into the Romantic mode, but I was never moved by the Diabelli like I am by the Goldbergs. It was good, but hardly more of the same, and certainly not a cut above. For every time I've listened to the Diabelli, I've probably heard the Goldbergs 20 times. Maybe more. This is not to denigrate Beethoven, but to merely state that this kind of thing is not the high point for him that it is for Bach.

When we speak of the Goldberg Variations, one name connected with them stands out above all the rest – Glen Gould.

When it comes to Gould, you are either an adulator or an ignorer. No middle ground exists. You can't be indifferent to Glen Gould unless you are indifferent to piano playing itself. I'm in the adulator ranks.

I don't know when I first became aware of Glen Gould, but I do know that the first entire recording I heard of the Goldbergs was a scratched lp of Gould's 1955 release purchased at a library sale in the 1980s. It was a disk that had been in circulation and then withdrawn. You could tell that many people had handled it and, probably even, listened to it.

I'd like to say that I "got it" the first time I played it. I knew by reputation that this was an important recording of an important composition before I put the needle on the lp, but it took a while for it to percolate inside me. When the cd set, "A Sense of Wonder" came out with both the 1955 and 1981 recordings by Gould of this work, I really got hold of it. Since then, I've heard other artists play it as well as transcriptions for other instrumental forces. It is a piece I never grow tired of listening to.

Gould played this as if he were a direct conduit back to Bach. I don't think in terms of the distinctions Gould thought of when he played the individual variations as he expressed them in some recorded interviews, but that's because it's not the technical aspects which speak to me, but the music in its entirety in and of itself.

Music is more than a succession of notes played in arrangements to one another at certain intervals. It is the whole which is created by composer, piece and performer. I think that's one reason I am so critical of 4'33". Anyone who can read a clock and "perform" this piece. The "composer" John Cage merely set a time frame, labeled his piece and left the performer to be still for that time frame. If anything occurs, it occurs in the mind of the audience. Bach knew better than that. He knew that the reception of the listener began with the ideas of the composer. Something has to be thrown before you can catch.

Bach connects directly with the mind across every cultural and language barrier. This is music functioning at its highest possible level. This is music demonstrating its communication superiority.

Language is based on a limited number of sounds forming an understood number of words or word roots. While it seems infinite, it can only be carried so far until what you get is Jabberwocky. The words are recognizable functionally as verbs and nouns, but all sense of their meaning is out the window, and each reader can make his own interpretation of it which will not connect him with another person.

Listeners sometimes make different things of what is heard, but, for all that, it is still in concrete. It is **something** regardless of what is "done" with it. Before I can make use of music, someone has to make it.

Plainchant is the starting point for our knowledge of Western music. No one really knows anything before that for certain. You might think that a limited number of tones sung in pretty much a steady monotone intensity would be a dead end to an art from, yet the release of the "Chant" album a few decades ago showed otherwise. Everyone sat up and took a second look at the entire genre. Anything with such a powerful beginning is sure to come to something. I don't know how much Bach might have known about chant, but he understood firmly rooting your music in words and tones and thoughts. That is a characteristic shared by both Bach and the anonymous chants. Why did I bring this in here? Because you start with the simple and then you work it out to a greater beauty.

Multitudes of composers have done variations since the Goldbergs and probably many did them before then as well. What Bach did was to explore the variety in a way which was unparalleled.

He roots the variations in a tune which he sets before us at the beginning and returns to at the end. That concept in itself is important. Variations have to vary from something, and that something has to be known. Bach always wrote in a world of absolute objective reality. We know where we begin and when we have ended. The work is a complete circle coming around to itself, containing everything within one framework, not letting it stray off.

We have every possible emotional tone set in this work. There is heaviness and lightness, joy and angst, power and seeming inconsequence. It's the kind of work that could be put on a tape loop. Even when it ends, it could be started again in the next breath of the player. It is telling us that life is different than what it was when we started out, and it changes along the way, but it always comes to sense.

I said that he rooted the variations in a tune. It could also be said that he works off a tune. So many times we don't get things done because we don't know where to start or, at the other end of things, we don't know how to end. Other times we have a starting point, but we don't know how to go or where to go. We don't know what to do with it. Bach knew beginning, middle and ending.

Some of the greatest works I've never written have suffered from simply not making a start. I wanted to do something, but that's all it turned out to be – a wanting which was wanting. Bach was never afraid to make a beginning. His beginnings are always deliberate, and none moreso than the Goldbergs.

We hear this work, once begun, adding variation to variation like stringing pearls for beauty or building with stones or bricks for strength. We could possibly imagine some arrangement or re-arrangement to an order to our liking, but we always see that variety is good. It is powerful. It is life.

Music needs to be put to work. It shouldn't be closeted away. When you have something good, don't just keep it on a shelf. Turn it around. Try it out with other things. Pick up the pace. Slow it down. One of the values of variety is that if you produce enough variations, you're sure to speak to everyone's hearts sooner or later. Variation enables us to look beyond the confines of our present emotional, intellectual or operational schematics. It helps us in our work and lives and will make us more interesting and accessible to others.

There is nothing more interesting than change. We don't always all like it, but we are all always interested in it. "New and Improved" doesn't pack the same wallop it used to pack on a product since the phrase has been used so much, but when something is new and we're not told about it, but discover it through our own experience, we wake up.

There was never a piece for waking people up like this one. I can't imagine dozing off with it. It's not turbulent, but it's not sleepy-peaceful, either. It arouses and retains the interest in a way that neither 4'33" nor the infamous "Bolero" do. (I guess that's enough bashing of Cage and Ravel.) Probably I could tell better if I had the score in front of me with every variation side by side, but there just doesn't seem to be any repeating here. It's the repetition which does us in. It drones and we cease to listen to the content and start grasping the form which is smooth and without a hand hold. Variance doesn't have to be large, but it gives us something to climb on.

Bach brings us back around to the tune at the end. As I've been listening to this just now, it caught me off guard. I didn't realize the count had reached the 30 variations. The very number of them didn't seem to matter. There was no clock-watching type approach, ticking them off so I could know when I arrived at the end. When I got to the end, there was peace and a rest, but also the knowledge that there was more and will continue to be more.

I'll play it again and see what comes this time.

New can become an end in itself, but this is more than an end. It is a constant beginning. The people at Athens were always discussing what was new according to Acts 17:21. That commentary seems true with regard to what we know about Greek culture. They were always moving beyond in their thinking. While there were probably some dead end thinkers in antiquity, the ones we hear about were always the restless ones, the ones looking for new frontiers in thought, not to define, but to cross. Bach takes us further, not because there is a virtue in that, but because, with a nod to Shakespeare's "more things in heaven and earth", there is more out there than we have imagined.

There is a sense in which we are always traveling in this life, but never arriving at the real and true end. We experience events along the way. There are new jobs, marriages, children, grandchildren, disappointments, joys, pains, promotions, achievements, but compared to what is to come they are same old same old. This lifetime is going somewhere; it will have an end. We are not living a one sided Mobius strip existence. We need something that will keep life fresh. Music does that.

This music is always fresh. It's always growing. It always has something more to say. Other compositions are often exhausted in the listening to or performing of them. They are what they are. I'm not criticizing. I listen to a lot of composers besides Bach, but none which is as universal as he is.

If nothing else, he proves here that music is not merely passing the time or taking up an occupation despite everyone telling you that you should study for a "real" profession. It means something in itself and the listening to it is meaningful.

The depth of the variety means that we can come back again and again without either satiety or disappointment. We're never stuffed with it. I suppose Gould might have gotten tired of playing it, although after giving up the concert stage in the 60s for exclusively performing via media, he didn't have to do the same pieces over and over anymore. Still, he showed that he couldn't get away from this piece. Just as it started his career in the wider world, so it ended it. He came back.

The second time he took longer, yet it's not that the piece was slowed down. As he pointed out in a radio interview, some of it was even faster the second time than it had been in 1955. When you can do something different with something familiar and get away with it, you prove that it is alive. Maybe, though, the work proves that you are alive.

I just came to a pause between variations in my listening. I almost hold my breath during the playing. These breaks remind me to breathe again. The work is not a single sentence lasting thirty-seven to sixty-seven or more minutes, depending on the playing speed of the pianist. It is a series. It is a group of steps we take whether we are playing or listening. We go from one to the next. Sometimes we skip. Other times we walk slowly, but always we are on the move. And just about the time the work seems to be leading us to taking a nap, it rises up and stirs us up.

Bach knew that variety was not just the spice of life; it was life. We breathe in; we breathe out. We sleep; we wake. We work; we rest. There is rhythm to all these, but variety takes it from an assembly line mode to a creative world of possibilities and blessings and joys.

The music always carries us. It never leaves us still. It is not a two way conversation between composer and performer, but an open party line in which the listener engages with the other two.

That's why Bach can prove things to me. He has made room for me in his music. The variations numbered thirty, but the variety of listeners is always increasing as the population of the world increases.

I could go on – and on – but, I think I will stop here for the moment. After all, there are other pieces to listen to.

But, I'll be back.

In <u>You Have To Love It</u> I wrote the following in the chapter in which I was describing what to me were the greatest works of various genres:

THE GREATEST INSTRUMENTAL WORK: Bach's Preludes and Fugues for the Well-Tempered Clavier

I put these above the Goldbergs, not because they are longer, but because they cover so much more ground. I have listened to several recordings by several different pianists, but I don't imagine I could say I have mastered them in that I don't always know what's going to come next. It's amazing how Bach's music can continue to be so fresh.

There's that word, fresh, again. For someone who died 201 years before I was born, he continues to be fresh. How is that possible?

It's because Bach is about inclusiveness. Very few things in life are all-inclusive, but Bach managed to be. He wrote music for his family and for his church, but I don't think he wanted it to stop there. He wrote for the world.

The Well-Tempered Clavier was written to a certain degree to champion an instrument which was trying to enter the world of music at the time and showcase it's possibilities. Bach was thinking ahead, and to give him credit, the keyboard has become one of the pre-eminent basic instruments in the Western world. I think Bach proved its worthiness, but along the way he proved other things as well.

The first thing I notice is distinctness here as against the homogeneity of the Goldbergs. Those are variations of a single theme to which they return, but these are not connected in that way. They take off every which way for 48 points of the compass. Each one stands on its own merits as a representative of a unique key in the collection.

We have differentiation and inclusion. We are not all one thing, nor do we have to be one thing. While I understand that Bach was something of an autocrat in running his choirs, his compositions speak of a broader base, although I wonder if he would have approved of all the playing techniques and styles that have been applied to them over the centuries.

This could be called "Plurality In Music". We speak a great deal about cultural and legal plurality, but usually most of us like our way best and don't care whether anyone else gets their way. Bach proves that music can be created in more directions than one.

As a composer, I have my own favorite keys in which I write. They are F, C, D, and G. Some of them are used because they are easier to play in. F is the most used because it allows me to go above the home point and below it, but when I'm done, I can sing a note that I can hit solidly which won't sound strained or faked from either end of the spectrum.

One year my wife talked about how I didn't have much variety in my keys, so I gave her some. Actually, I did more than what she wanted when I decided to write a set of songs in as many keys as I could. We had a two week Vacation Bible School that year. I wrote a theme song and ten additional songs, one for each day. At the end, I had eleven songs in eleven different keys. What did I learn from that?

The timing and intervals between the notes are the same in whatever key you write, but the difficulty to the piano player increases with more sharps or flats employed, although certainly the average singer wouldn't notice it when singing.

Writing in some of these strange keys made me become more inventive at times, and I did things I wouldn't have done if I had stayed in my old favorite keys. I won't say I learned this from Bach, although I had a recording of the first Well-Tempered Clavier book before I wrote these songs. Certainly the fact that Bach had done what he had done was a trailblazing effect showing that it could be done. There was a variety there that was missing from some of my other songs written in that same era.

I don't think I'd attempt anything so comprehensive again, although if I did, I would go all the way and attempt all 24 keys to say that I had done what Bach did. I don't know that Bach did this more than doing the second series. It's as if he then said, "Now, it's up to you to carry it out." What he proved, though, was invaluable. Increased difficulty calls for increased ingenuity. It gets one out of the rut and brings life to the music. It breaks up the monotonous sameness and lets invention abound.

No artist's work should end with himself. Bach's doesn't. Pianists learn the various keys and their values by playing these works. While listeners don't always experience the strengths and weaknesses and distinctives of the various keys in the way a player would, they can be nurtured by the beauty of the art.

Bach is opening the door to music in an even greater way than he did with any other specific work. This excels The Art of the Fugue which concentrates more specifically on form alone. This has form, too. There is a prelude and fugue in every key, but I never think "form" when I listen to the Well-Tempered Clavier. I only think "music". There is a breadth in that category of "music" which encompasses not only the art, but us as well.

I believe that in these two sets of compositions Bach was attempting to prove that music could be made in every key and in every kind of key. I don't know if it would even be possible to have something besides major and minor, but if it had been, Bach would have written in it. Ultimately, he shows that music can inhabit many different kinds of spaces. If the key changes, so can the chords and the other structural elements. There are always places to go in music.

All approaches to music are valid. I once heard someone speak who distinguished between chords and notes and intervals and rhythms, declaring some to be wrong in and of themselves. No one who knows music would ever think that. That doesn't mean that everything which is said in music is edifying, anymore than everything written in the English language is. People misuse both language and music, but there is nothing in musical forms or keys which are moral or immoral in and of themselves. A rhythm structure or key signature is neutral. That's the point. While we may need to be discerning on the meaning the composer is intending to put in certain music, there just is no such thing as a bad note or timing element. Syncopation is not sinful.

I've consumed a lot of music by composers whose personal philosophies and lives and theologies I disagree with. This is because the music itself has a value distinct from their philosophic platform, and I am free to experience it for itself without implying any approval of the beliefs of the composer or performer. Even dissonance has a value, but it is no equal to the value of tonalism. No one can believe in nothing. Something is there, and it has an objective existence. Bach knew that above all as we'll see in the next chapter.

Bach proves the value of all music to speak to us. We are not to be limited to certain keys or forms. We can come to music with complete freedom. We come knowing that no one is excluded and that, even though someone's creation doesn't fit what has come so far, no one should be squelched. There is greater freedom here than in any other art form. Those are limited by the materials out of which they are constructed. Music has only the limitation of the mind.

We live in a world filled with exclusions. In some societal settings it is more important who not to invite than it is who to invite. Lucy made that very clear to Charlie Brown when she said there must have been a mix-up in the lists as he wasn't supposed to have been invited to the Halloween party.

Bach does not want to exclude anyone or anything. I have no idea how many of these keys he wrote in on a regular basis or if he wrote in all equally, but it doesn't matter. We know that he did it at least twice in every case. No one can accuse Bach of narrowness.

Liberal is a term which is bandied about quite a bit. Politically we have defined it in a certain way, but the word itself has nothing to do with a particular platform. It means to be free and open and generous. When we use the word liberal, we are speaking in an absolute sense of breadth and freedom and open-mindedness rather than in the sense of a particular political viewpoint. Liberality is, above all, generous.

Bach was liberal. He was open to the influences of other composers, but mostly he was open to music. I don't think he ever knew ahead of time where it was going to take him. I don't mean he didn't have a structure, but as I listen to these pieces I can sense a movement of thinking and not a static mind unable to go beyond the confines of set pathways.

The multiplicity of keys proves that we should, likewise, be open. I know that Western music has arrived at these 24 keys (the major and minor of each of the 12 tones), but that is not a limit. It is merely a way of working with the instruments which we have. It's good not to try to be too innovative, though. We couldn't possibly keep up with a system in which every new instrument maker introduced a different number of keys in which the tones changed. There would be no capability of interface between such a collection of instruments. A always has to be 440, at least that's what it's established as in the concert hall for the most part. If we start to mess around with that, instrumentalists will no longer be able to play in concert. We will have noise instead of music. We will be left with uncertainty. Bach is always certain. He knows what he is doing and what his music is doing. He wants us to be certain, too.

Within the realm of the 24 keys, there are an infinite number of possibilities. The Well-Tempered Clavier proves that by itself, but it does not declare itself to be the end of music, only a launching point for it.

Every time I think I have discovered all that there is to discover in music, I find a different composer or a new (to me) piece which opens up my thinking. Bach is an introduction to others as well as to himself.

The BBC Music Magazine has a feature which analyzes the available recordings on a particular prominent work each month. They give their estimate of the best, along with some runners up and one to avoid. Then on the next page they make, "If you liked that, you might like this" suggestions. That can be helpful. Even with a listener of broad experience, there is always going to be some work he doesn't know of which would go well in his schematic or which would broaden it out. Music is far beyond our limitations of it.

Bach in this work begs us to like music, rather than to like Bach. I always come back to Bach, but having known him, I am encouraged to explore further shores while at the same time I have a safe harbor to come back to.

There is a place for every person in music. There is a place for every emotion and every thought. There is a key which will fit somewhere in there.

Other music is closed in upon itself. It demands allegiance to a form or period or style, but Bach is universal. He didn't write his music to build a fence around us, but to show us what could be done with 12 notes and a heart to make music with them.

I have my favorite keys, but in so doing I am validated by Bach. He could do something in every key. I can do something in the ones I use. It's not the keys, but what we do with them that is important. Do we regard them as boundaries or do we make music through them?

I believe that Bach would want us to go forth and multiply.

Like the moon depicted on the front cover, Bach reflects the direct light of God. His light could only shine if God's light shone before it.

What we do, we do by the direction in which we are pointed.

Bach proves the power and fruit of the dedicated life. It's not that every life which is dedicated will be able to compose like Bach did, but that **Bach** did what **he** did by this dedication, and we know what **he** did. We are not talking about the result of Bach's music, but the pointed direction of it.

Many people are greatly concerned with the concept of orientation in areas of morals and politics. They judge others by their own standards. Bach didn't judge anyone but himself. Not only that, he didn't need a G P S for spatial orientation. He had another set of letters to go by.

We have already pointed out that no one can believe in nothing. No one is a vacuum. Everyone does believe in something. Even people who claim to have no beliefs at all believe in unbelief. This kind of nihilism is not very productive usually, either for the individual or for society.

The entire orientation of Bach's life can be summed up in three letters. With these he signed his manuscripts. They were the completion of each piece of work.

S D G. The Latin initials for Soli Deo Gloria.

Why do we do what we do? Is it for money? Is it for the convenience? Is it to receive acclaim for doing it? Is it because we have an irresistible "I Gotta Be Me" impulse to do it?

What Bach did, he did for Someone else. He gave the credit for his work to the One who had worked and authored him. A person could revel in his own creations, especially those such as Bach created. He could expect to bask in the adulation of others. He could make a name for himself. None of that was true of Bach, not when he used those initials.

I know enough of Latin to know that these three words mean **Only** **God** **Glory**. Only God is to get the glory. Only God is where the glory goes. Only God possesses or has the glory. Whatever words you supply in between to make English sentence sense, you get the fact that there is something about glory which goes only to or with God.

Only is a word of exclusivisity. It excludes everything outside the class being spoken of. It is a word of singleness. One is not a lonely number; it is a complete number. There's nowhere else that glory could go than to God as there is nowhere else which glory comes from than God.

Bach did not think in terms of pluralism when it came to this. He didn't think about spreading the wealth so that everyone gets credit. Once in 8th grade (over 50 years ago), the teacher divided us up into teams to give oral presentations on social studies topics. Ours had to do with the influence of communism in America. This was in the 60s, so we were past the red scare, but there was still a lot of concern about communism. I mention this, not because it matters, but to show what my memory was of this event and how I felt about it.

We had met in committee and divided up the topic. I went to the library and found what I could on my part of the presentation. The day came for our report. I had a lot of notes and had mimeographed some papers to hand out. I don't remember how many there were in our group, but not a single other person in the group had done any research at all. They then proceeded to pressure me into dividing up what I had done among them so that they would have something to present. I gave in and let them have it, but the whole time I was angry and felt it was wrong. I wasn't out for glory, but I felt as though the credit for my work was being stolen from me. There was a sense of violation. I'm long over that, and I couldn't even tell you the names of the people involved, but I cite it as an illustration of the injustice when several people take credit for one person's work.

We often give glory where it doesn't belong. Celebrityism is a plague both in and out of the church. Sometimes people aren't even glorified for any actual accomplishments, but for their charismatic personality alone, which is almost the same as glorifying us for our choice of them to glorify.

Glory does not originate inside us. It is not a prize we bestow on the world. There is no opinion poll that creates it. It stands firm in and of itself. It comes from and goes where it belongs. A glory which does not will disappear.

Now, we should not think that God is the least bit prideful, but in Isaiah 42:8, God made it very clear that He would give His glory to no others. This is one time when He won't share, and He is right not to share. It wouldn't be in accordance with the truth, and it might give people the wrong ideas about idols or false gods which would lead to eternal loss. Glory is for God alone.

Bach knew that. He may or may not have known how basic his music was or was going to prove to be, but he knew that ONLY God was to get the glory from it.

God was not an ill-defined amorphous concept for Bach. God was not an eastern all-soul becoming. God was not one of a thousand personalities. God was not a being who appeared in a story once told to explain things, but who is no longer believed in. Bach's God and mine is the Yahweh of the Old Testament who came in the flesh as Jesus Christ in the New Testament and who has been further revealed as the Holy Spirit dwelling in the saints and in the church.

God created us and then re-created us. These actions show the fame of God and His renown to be deserved. Light can be re-directed by mirrors or other objects, but it only radiates from one place. As bright as the moon can be at times, no one who has ever seen the sun will mistake the moon for the sun. The moon is reflected glory. It can never be anything else. The sun is the real thing. Only the one who can deliver the goods can get the glory.

Glory is a word of fame, of renown. It is like a light shining out from the one who has it. It radiates from God and what He has done, but it should also flow to Him from His people. Either way, only He is to have it.

Neither the music nor Bach himself belonged to Bach. They both belonged to God. This is why Bach signed his music with his declaration of the glory of God.

Bach is not merely the greatest musician and composer who ever lived; he is also one of the greatest Christians who ever lived. According to <u>The Bach Reader</u> he could be hard to get along with at times, and, like many musicians, he had to struggle to get his funeral honorariums, for example, but it is his orientation in life which defines him and his art. It is true of all his music, not merely that which has scriptural themes. All of it was given to God. Do we give everything to God?

In a way, it is not that we give God anything, but that He alone has everything, and we don't look for it anywhere else. We acknowledge rather than bestow glory.

Glory always gets a person's attention. This is where Bach wanted our attention to be, not on lesser things. It's where he himself focused. He was lined up on the glory of God. When we are lined up there, we have the proper orientation.

Bach proves that we are not alone, that we are not here by chance, that we are not without resources, that we have an open window for redemption, that peace is a real possibility. All by these three letters. His music has the calm confidence of trust in God which I don't always hear from other composers. I'm not trying to start an index of godly vs. non-godly composers. I'm not really saying anything against anyone else, only about Bach. And even those who do not acknowledge God often have value in their music for they live in the same world Bach lived in, whether they want to acknowledge it or not.

Where we orient ourselves is important for ourselves and also for others, for they often follow the path we make. We should live our lives in such a way that at the end of them we arrive somewhere and others who follow arrive there, too.

Unless you aim at something, you will hit nothing. Bach chose the largest target of all, and he went where he aimed. I believe it so much that I can say that one day I will see him and possibly speak with him. I say that tentatively as I don't believe in either the floating on clouds or old home week approaches to what the experience of heaven will be. We don't know, probably not because God is unwilling to tell us, but because we are unable to understand at the present time exactly how it will be, but we know it will be beyond anything we've ever experienced.

With regard to you, though, your orientation governs your life and your destiny, no one else's. It only works, if as in Bach's case, what you are oriented toward is really there and is provides you with a benefit for going to it. These three letters provide a point of reference to the absolute. When we look at a map we can't make sense of it without knowing which way is north. These letters show us where we came from and where we are going.

S D G is also an anchor. It attaches us to someone larger than we are. It keeps us safe in the storm. Sometimes people talk about riding on someone else's coattails. We can't get anywhere other than on God's coattails.

These three letters are not only where Bach gave the credit, but they also provided a reason. If what you do is going to be lost, you don't have much motivation to do it. Though some of Bach's works were lost on this earth, they were never lost to God. He doesn't wait for them to be discovered in some long forgotten library. He has them in His heart where they will never be lost. That's not only reason to do something, but it is reason to do the best that you can do.

Bach gave God the glory for no one else. He merely showed where his own focus and interests lay, and in so doing he proclaimed a path which could be followed.

It's interesting though, that it wasn't always followed to the same degree. I know that times change and what was the musical fashion one day becomes the "old" fashioned the next. I've read that that's how Bach's own sons regarded their father's music. I've been hearing some things recently by C. P. E. Bach, one of the more prominent sons, and I've noticed that the intensity which was in his father's work doesn't seem to be there in his. I haven't heard his complete corpus, so I can't comment on everything, and also so much depends on the fire or lack of it with which the instrumentalists play the music on the recordings I've heard, but I don't think I'll probably ever get a complete set of C. P. E., not when there are more sets of J. S. out there.

I don't see Bach's own intensity in other later composers.

Haydn had his Sturm und Drang period and Beethoven re-introduced intensity like it had never been introduced before, but it wasn't like Bach's. It was a force of music and of personality, but not a personality based on the absolute conviction of S D G.

Composers, because they are human beings made in the image of God, can create beauty and power in their music apart from God because of that very image they are molded in. On the other hand, some who have a total sense of the glory of God can't carry a tune in a bucket with the lid nailed down, as I've heard it put. God gets the glory because he made both kinds. Everything we do comes home to roost in Him one way or another.

Bach was able to create and create in power and light. I believe it was because of his orientation and the fact the light of God shone on and through him. That's what glory can do, and only God has the glory that can do it.

If entropy is king, as scientists claim, we are living in a world characterized by diminishing power. Even if the universe is expanding as some claim, it is expanding to thinner dimensions than before. It is scattering and dissipating. Everything is getting farther away. Everything is losing ground. Configurations are changing and connections are lost. The constellations will need to be renamed, and man may have to find a new home on another planet along the lines of the science fiction stories. Each day is better than the next in such a world which many think is destined one day to collapse in upon itself of its own weight.

But, that's not the world Bach lived in or believed in.

God is powerful. Thoughts are powerful. Bach wanted to proclaim these powers. He wanted to express himself through and in the most powerful medium of his day. The organ was and is the most powerful **single** musical instrument.

The Organ!!!!

Many people don't like it. They think it's passé or depressing or too heavy. Some are frightened by it. Others are bored by it. Yet, it has power that no other single instrument has. This has been believed even into modern times as we witness in the Saint-Saens third symphony. The orchestra plays along for a long time and the symphony is good. Then the organ jumps in and the balance is overwhelmingly on the organ's side, and the symphony, it becomes great.

This is one of the oldest instruments which is in use at the present time. It predates the piano by centuries. You would think that in all that time it's potential would have been fully used up. Bach considered all the evidence and pronounced a verdict of "Not Proven" to that idea.

Bach was intimately acquainted with the organ. From all that I've read, it was **his** instrument. He was known as a tester and critic of new organs. He would often be hired to come in and put them through their paces to discover their weaknesses and their strengths. If anyone knew what the organ was capable of, it was

Bach. And, if anyone was able to take the organ where it had never been taken before, it was Bach. He made the organ and his music for it iconic.

This interest had been with him from the beginning. We alluded earlier to his walking to hear Buxtehude. Some people grow out of their early enthusiasms. Not Bach. If he left the organ behind, it was only because he was leading it to places it had never been before.

Power is often used to frighten. Some people even do that with Bach's music as it or music like it is so often played in scary movies to put us in "the mood" for being frightened, but it was meant to put us in a state of awe for someone greater than us.

There is a difference between fearing God and being afraid of Him. When Adam walked with God in the garden before eating the fruit of the tree of the knowledge of good and evil, he feared God. He gave God his proper respect and attention. He treated God with the deference that was due Him by obeying Him and fellowshipping with him. After Adam ate, he was afraid of God. He hid from God. He could not face this One he had so disrespected with his disobedience.

If we understand Bach's music correctly, rather than frightening, it should embolden us. Through Jesus Christ we can stand in the presence of God. We do not have to keep quiet or still or so efface ourselves that God will not notice us. We can speak freely.

God is a God of power and He is approached in power through music. As Adam walked side by side with God in the garden, so God wants the saint to walk side by side with Him in worship and prayer and in every day life on this earth.

Whenever the organ plays, it dominates. I have not heard this music played very often by a live organist because the churches I am a part of don't use this level of music. The times I have heard it in person, though, it is something more than "background music". It doesn't give the option of ignoring it. You have to pay attention to the organ, just as you should pay attention to God.

On the other hand, the organ is able to lighten down to

almost inaudibility at times. Even then it still dominates because I find myself cocking my ear and thinking, "What's it doing now?" There's the expectation that it is going to pick things up again and go back to where it was and probably beyond. I don't think any other instrument is capable of being as loud and as soft as the organ can be. At the loud end we can barely think. At the soft end we can barely hear. It's almost as if the vibrations alone are speaking to us, but it is telling us of the completeness which is there. It is almost the alpha and omega of musical instruments.

Potential seems to be powerful, but we often discount it because it's turned out to be the opposite so often. When you actually try to get into the sky, you find out how ephemeral the castles you built there are. The organ is potential realized. What it imagines, it delivers.

A great, good reality exists. The world shouts at us that it does not. The organ drowns out the world. It keeps us from despair. While the organ in its "frightening" aspects seems to foster despair, through Bach it is really calling us to abandon despair. It speaks with a voice which cannot be ignored. It says that Might rules discouragement, and that the might of God is for you. Bach's music is never an attack on anyone. It is power employed for them. Listen to any of Bach's organ works all the way to its end; you will never come away hopeless.

The organ digs deep inside of us. When it plays, we have the soul out in the open. Maybe that's why it's unsettling. We feel more naked before the organ than before any other musical instrument or ensemble. It's as though the music can see right through us. It leaves nothing hidden. We are penetrated and exposed. Rather than discovering the music, the music discovers us. That may be too subjective of an approach, but it explains some of what happens when we hear the organ music of Bach. (I don't make this claim for the music of a theater organ or the normal church organ playing "Rock Of Ages".) Knowing this, I don't think a person will start to like organ music if they haven't liked it before, but perhaps the frightening element will be removed from it.

The most familiar organ work of Bach's is the Toccata and

Fugue in D minor. It is one of the best known classical pieces in the repertoire and probably the most famous organ piece of all time. Whenever it starts, no matter how many times I've heard it, I mentally sit up and take notice. I know where we're going and even when we're going there and what the sequence will be, but that makes me more interested rather than less. I've heard it played with a heavy hand and with a lighter touch. But either way, it is power.

I think the great thing about the D minor is not that it is power in itself, but that I feel the power growing inside me when I hear it. If ever a piece of music swelled up inside a person's heart, this is it. There are a places where it struggles, and the struggle element is important. We don't want to think that power is easy. Even our God Himself struggled for us. There is no abrasion between us and God, but there is seriousness. He takes us seriously. Can we ask anything more of Him to begin with?

The organ music of Bach has brought out great organists. One of the most famous of the 20th century to champion Bach was Albert Schweitzer. I've only heard one recording of his playing, and it's pretty scratchy. By today's standards it seems rather subdued, but that may just be from the limited amount of selections on the one recording. It seems that he plays a little more precisely and not as freely as other professional organists whose recordings I've heard. This could be because he didn't have as much time to spend with the music as they did. Still, I see this as demonstrating the power of the music and the instrument. A man who was famous in theology and medicine and humanitarian work gave himself to Bach's music as well, showing its place firmly in life.

E. Power Biggs is the other large name associated with Bach's organ works. I've heard a recording of his playing the D minor. It, too, is a little more controlled than some of the more recent recordings I've heard, but he had a full mastery of the instrument and the piece. He was not just playing the notes, but playing his heart. That's what organists do, and I have a feeling it takes more out of them to do it than any other instrument does.

Every time one of Bach's pieces is played on the organ,

even by unbelievers, the power of God is proclaimed. You can like the music for itself, but it speaks of Him every time, regardless of the intentions of the player. Bach is not forcing anyone to glorify God, but if they choose to use music written for that purpose, their use of it will not change its focus. It will always be what it is.

We are weak many times, but there is strength, there is power, and it's for us. The fact that his music is still played and recorded by our greatest organists shows that Bach continues to prove the power.

7 Interface With The World

To turn around an old saying, Bach demonstrates that while we are not of the world, we are in the world, and we can make them know it.

Music can take you anywhere. It can connect you with anyone. It can bridge gaps and communicate with people you could never speak to, either linguistically or socially. Bach proved that it could be done because he did it. Even though he was oriented toward heaven, he was able to speak to this world.

Interface with the world is good and profitable, providing we are influencing the world and not being dragged down by it. Bach did the influencing without suffering for it.

The Musical Offering seems to be an almost unique event in Bach's music and in the classical repertoire as a whole. It shows that he was not merely cloistered away with his choir and his instruments, but that he was at home in the world. Certainly you had to be out there in order be even known by, much less received by, one of the most well known political and military figures of your world.

Frederick the Great was great in his day (1712-1786), but his history hasn't caused him to come down to our day as well known as rulers such as Louis XIV or Napoleon or leaders such as Washington or Lincoln. To most of us, he is little more than a name. I have read a lot of history, but I couldn't give you any kind of outline off the top of my head or his achievements or aims. His greatest impact may not have been set down in changes in the colors on the map, but in a great encounter with Bach which bore great fruit.

Bach was not the cosmopolite that Handel was. He lived and worked in what was a very small circle. He didn't run around making a name for himself. But his name was known by those far outside the circle of his venue of employment and his labors.

Frederick gave Bach the tune himself. He was a musician in his own right. I have heard one piece by him, although I can't say that it is particularly outstanding or memorable, but still it was real music. The tune he gave Bach probably travelled farther than anything Frederick could have written himself. There's a lesson in that. We should not be self-concerned with our creations. Sometimes we need to let others do something with what we have which could go beyond where we can go. Bach took what Frederick gave him and created the "Musical Offering".

Music is designed for others. Many of us play for our own enjoyment, and it can be a kind of therapy, but ultimately music must be for others. Usually, the musician feels sorrow when his music is <u>not</u> heard.

Bach called it an "Offering". That specifies its character. It was never meant to be hoarded or gloried in as an example of "how good I am", but it was designed to be given. This is music which was meant to build others up. I'm not aware of another major composition by any composer which is called an offering. This seems to be something which Bach did which no one else did. At least if they did do it (which I wouldn't be surprised at) they didn't do it in such a way as leave a legacy as Bach did in this work.

I think when I first got a copy of The Musical Offering I was expecting a single work or perhaps a unified suite of some kind. What I got was a collection of pieces of various lengths and even various instrumentation. Bach's greatness wasn't limited to works of great scope such as the St. Matthew Passion or the Well-Tempered Clavier. He exhibited his strength in the smallest of places as well.

Here Bach shows how you can start with a snippet provided by someone else and build something beautiful. He wasn't so concerned with being "original" as he was with being good. He took what **he** was given and made something which he then gave back.

We can make something out of almost anything. The important thing is to fashion it for the joy and edification of others. If we spend all our time trying to achieve the "perfect" piece or the perfect anything, we have lost sight of the fact that what we do is for others, not to further our own glory. Bach had already taken care of that possibility in his continued use of S D G. He could be free because this was done for God's glory, not his own.

This world is destined to perish, yet it provides points of contact. We should not despise, but use them to reach out. Everyone is always pleasantly surprised to find something he knows. We say that we don't like "old hat", but we're comfortable with the familiar, and nothing is so familiar as something we have thought up ourselves. I'm not condoning plagiarism, but if we show that we can do something with what someone else has to offer (as the tune was offered to Bach), we do a great thing.

Very few of us could do what Bach did musically, and with all the copyright constrictions today we could not do what he did without permission, usually, but we can take a compliment which is given to us and re-fashion it and pass it on. We can take a blessing from someone else and pronounce it over another. We can pass along a good deed, a smile, a prayer, a gift, a personal reminiscence.

We were not designed to be dead ends. We were not created to be getters, but givers. Bach demonstrates that here.

Also, Bach proves that we don't have to be boisterous or harsh with the world to get its attention. We can hardly imagine anything in this work as an abrasive attack. Bach treats us gently and with deference and respect. This doesn't mean that we are fools and let ourselves be taken advantage of, but that as far as it depends on us, we will be at peace will all men as Paul put it in Romans 12:18.

Bach had many connections with the world. Although not as many as his sacred cantatas, he did write a number of secular ones. The one I have been most fascinated with is the "Coffee Cantata". I originally had it on a Nonesuch lp with the "Peasant Cantata" on the flip side. I don't know that the music was particularly exceptional, but I was fascinated by the fact that Bach would write a work about a woman who insisted on having more coffee than her father thought was good for her, if my memory of the back liner notes serves me. I don't know where or when it was performed or what occasioned its composition, but it gives a whimsical letting off of steam to balance the heavier works of Bach. It honors the every day nature of our lives.

We are people in the world with our own interests. The beverage seems so much a part of our world as to be thoroughly uncontroversial. It doesn't even seem like there would be such a problem in today's world.

I have to limit own daily coffee intake, not because of the caffeine, but because it is high in oxalates which could form a kidney stone in me. Still, I can't imagine doing an entire musical work on my medical saga, culminating with the moment when the doctor handed me the list of "bad" foods which I should avoid on which would appear most prominently to my utter horror the word coffee and getting away with it like Bach got away with this.

The "Coffee Cantata" has some importunate melodies which give it a more drama-dominated character than the sacred cantatas. It's a human produced drama, not a divine one.

Bach is telling us that sometimes families have to work things out. I'm not sure how it worked out in this case, as the set I have the work on now only has the German text, and I don't read German. But, in a way, it doesn't matter. It's the give and take which is important.

While we can't give in to everyone's preferences always, we should never squelch the person so as to diminish them. Drama doesn't have to end in tragedy. It can flatten out and come back to normal. The value of airing out these "differences" is that people should learn to know and respect one another. That's not usually what happens, but it is what should happen.

There are not nearly as many secular vocal works in the Bach catalogue as there are sacred ones. Some of them were recycled into sacred pieces such as the secular cantata music which ended up in the Christmas Oratorio with appropriate text. I read about that in the extensive booklet which came with the first recording I bought of the oratorio some twenty years ago. Then, when I got the complete set of Bach, I recognized the music immediately when I heard it in its original secular cantatas.

I don't see anything wrong with recycling your own output. Today, because of recording, we can hear that rather readily, but even into fairly recent times they wouldn't have always made the connection. People who had heard one outing of the music may not have heard the other, or, since they only heard it when performed and not at their own command as we listen to recorded music, they may not remember it.

I don't know if it worked the other direction, where Bach took a sacred piece and secularized it. I would imagine not, but I don't think Bach would have a problem sanctifying a secular piece, if it fit something he was called upon to do. Everything was up for being brought to the attention of God. Everything was fit for the edifying of others.

Others may have been sucked into the vortex of the world system, but Bach always kept his head above waters. We never hear anything which would imply that he changed his orientation. At the same time, because this music was used out in the world, it formed a bridge which could bring the listener over into the sacred realm.

We should not cut ourselves off from the world or move in isolation which doesn't touch it. Occasionally, the world "discovers" godly music as it did a few decades back in the "Chant" phenomenon, but normally they ignore it.

Bach was able to present something in a way in which it could not be ignored. I'm listening to the "Peasant Cantata" now. It doesn't seem to have the intensity of the "Coffee" or maybe it's just that it doesn't capture my attention in the way that the concept of a cantata written about coffee does, but it is still very pleasant music worth listening to.

The world listens to what it deems worthy of its attention. From time to time, works or recordings will have a runaway popularity unconnected with the music critics or recording industry powers, but usually they, the modern version of the patrons of old, control much of what we get to hear. If they don't think it's any good, they won't perform or record it. I know that not everything Bach wrote was a flash of lightening to dazzle and illuminate the entire world by its brilliance, but every thing was good, and if Bach could connect himself with the world through it, then that was to the good.

8 There Are Places For Individuals And Groups

Everyone longs for a place to feel at home in and from which to engage the world. Some work better alone; others work better as a part of a team. Neither one style is better or worse than the other. Music proves that.

I won't attempt to do an analysis of every instrument or grouping Bach wrote for, but the principles coming out of his music are worth knowing. That's why we never throw Bach out. Other cds may go to the thrift store or library sale, but not his.

Many composers did what we are going to talk about and continue to do it, but Bach really opened up personality in music. He may not have initiated it, but he certainly did it permanently. Bach equipped musicians in both solo and combined forces by the pieces he wrote for them, and he did it as it had never been done before. If you don't believe me, listen to something before him, and then listen to something after him. Pick anything you want, and you'll see what I mean. There is no rigidity to Bach such as you would hear in the era before him. I say that, realizing that we are depending on modern day performances of these works. No one alive can tell us what a performance by Bach or his predecessors was like. Even today, when it would seem that he should be crystallized into performance patterns, we see more variety than ever.

In his Passions and cantatas, Bach wrote for cooperation on a grand scale. We might think that since that was so important, he wouldn't bother with the individual, but he does. He gave us unaccompanied solo music for the clavier, the organ, the violin, the cello and the lute.

We've already examined some of the pieces for solo instruments such as the Well-Tempered Clavier, the Goldberg Variations and the Toccata and Fugue in D minor. Someone who had written only those pieces would stand in posterity, but Bach knew that as there were a wealth of players on a wealth of instruments, there must be a wealth of pieces for them.

Music is wealth. It's not capital to be kept in reserve, but a resource to be put into circulation to boost the cultural economy. What is shared reaches the farthest.

The violin has always been the most versatile stringed instrument. It leads in the orchestra. As a solo voice it has a great range and strength. It can capture the attention as Bach does in the solo sonatas and partitas. I have heard solo violin works by more contemporary composers, but none with the heart of Bach's.

The six cello suites are almost unparalleled in classical literature. Every time a new recording of these is released, it's announced with reverence and awe not given to recordings of other compositions. It's as if these suites deserve our attention. Others have used the cello powerfully in concertos or in symphonic forms, but the cello standing alone? Only Bach. He showed the excellence that could be achieved here.

The solo works have called out the greatest of our soloists: Gould, Leonhardt, Schweitzer, Biggs, Rostropovich, Segovia and multitudes of others. The works call for the best and they get it. If someone wants to aspire to being the best, he must climb the works of Bach to reach his goal.

The orchestra on its own had little place in Bach. When we think of his music, we don't think of the orchestra as we do in the cases of Beethoven or Brahms. Rather than an entity on its own, it is a platform for vocal and instrumental soloists to build upon. That is one of the things that music is supposed to do. It is to built cooperation among the players and unity among the listeners.

About all we have for the orchestra alone are the four Orchestral suites. I wonder what Bach would have done in the full scale symphony realm had it been a more developed form in his day. I once had an album that took some of the Sinfonias and overtures from the cantatas and presented them as an instrumental album. It was a good one even though the pieces were taken out of their original contexts. Maybe that says something. If you can remove a part of a piece from its milieu and still give joy, it must be good, and the ones on that recording were all good.

Personally, I wish Bach had left us some string quartets. I think the art form was in its infancy in his day. It wasn't until a generation or so later in Haydn that they came into their own. If Bach had taken the form in hand, though, it would have been something.

On a smaller scale, we have soloists combining among themselves or combining with larger ensembles to perform the keyboard concertos, violin concertos and sonatas, cello concertos, and flute concertos. The Musical Offering is a combination and solo and ensemble performances all under a single heading.

Then, there are **the Brandenburgs**.

I can't say enough about them, but I will testify to their greatness. The Brilliant people put them as the first recordings in their entire Bach set. I have acquired several other recordings of them over the years. One of the greatest things I ever heard in a concert setting was Jean Pierre Rampal playing one at the Hollywood Bowl with the Los Angeles Chamber Orchestra in the mid 1990s. Never before or since have I heard music playing like they did that night which made me feel like I was hearing heaven ahead of time.

Bach knew about synergy. He knew that by getting people to cooperate you had great musical forces. There is a power in harmony which multiplies melody into a great force. It is not the complication of the harmony, but the structural security of it that provides this power. Bach's interplay among the musicians provides that.

Both ensembles and soloists need to come to the concert. We need them both. Bach was no apostle of quietism. He wrote so that when his music was played individually, it would be forthright and powerful. He also showed how much could be done when we cooperate with others.

If we were all doing our utmost and, at the same time, helping others to do their utmost, we would have a world of beauty and function all at the same time, which leads us to the following.

9 You Can Work With Others And They Can Work With You

We don't usually think of cooperation in the composition of classical music.

Popular songs have many cooks working over the broth. Authors band together to produce books. Look at the list of names at the beginning of any standard college textbook. Engineering feats may begin in the mind of one person, but they almost always require the cooperation of many on both the drawing table and in the manufacturing to become reality.

Classical Music, is something usually done one person at a time. Other than working with librettists and the time he took a tune from Frederick the Great and worked it into the Musical Offering, I don't think Bach collaborated with anyone. Yet, he did something else. He showed that you could build something new and great on what someone else had done before.

I don't know that this is a complete list of the composers Bach borrowed from, but I do know that he reworked music from Vivaldi, Corelli, Marcello, Ernst, Telemann and Torelli in transcriptions. He did his own version of Pergolesi's "Stabat Mater". Composers freely "borrowed" from one another in the old days in a way that today would be prosecuted as copyright violation. In some ways, if they had not done that then, many of these works might not have come down to us at all for they would have been performed and the scores kept in only very restricted localities and have been subject to loss. Such work is not only a matter of cross-pollination, but also of preservation.

I first became aware of Bach's transcription work in an organ cd by Christopher Herrick. I bought the cds, not because they were transcriptions of anyone else's work, but because they were Bach. Finding out that I was getting what might be considered "used music" didn't lessen my enjoyment, but increased it, especially as I was already a Vivaldi follower. Two of my favorites had teamed up. The fact that both men had something of themselves in the same pieces made them even more valuable rather than less. Bach brought over some of the Italian brightness to the north. It was glorious.

I don't know that I recognized Vivaldi at first in the organ transcriptions, but I certainly did in the harpsichord transcriptions I heard in the Brilliant complete Bach set some years later. That recognition set me on familiar ground with a point of reference. Not that I have ever been lost in the music of Bach, but the familiar is always appealing. The brightness shines to a greater magnitude.

I have a recording of Pergolesi's "Stabat Mater" and also one of Bach's "Tilge, Hochster Meine Sunden" (BWV 1083) which is labeled "After Pergolesi's Stabat Mater".

Pergolesi's piece is great to begin with. I've not only heard it on recording, but I attended a concert in which it was presented in a live performance. I can't say that I know Pergolesi's work beyond this piece, but if a person could only write one piece, this is the kind of piece to write. It is a work of sheer beauty and makes up in quality what is not present in quantity in my collection.

Bach takes the work in hand and applies an even lighter touch than we have in the original. It's as if he fine tuned the sensitivity of the scene of Mary standing at the cross. I'm not saying that he makes it better or improves on it, but he takes a work from the south and translates it to the north where it may not have been as well known or had as ready an audience, and he does so without any northern heaviness.

It is as if Bach is standing by the composer, who had a short lifespan totally within the span of Bach's own life, and saying that he approves of this work. He does this by building out of pre-existing materials.

Actually, everyone does that in music. No one has an exclusive license to the middle C that we all use. Notes and time signatures and keys have all been countlessly recycled. In this case, it is a work which gains a new life. Bach took what was good in others and made it good in himself. He gave his best to what others had already given their best to.

One of the values of transcriptions is that they introduce people to music they might not have known otherwise. Rather than being a dead end, they show that music is a river which flows both to the past and the future. It never stands still.

In transcriptions the worth of those who preceded is acknowledged. No one would, of his own will, do a transcription of a piece of trash, although I suppose if they were being commissioned to do so, they might do it for the sake of the money involved. Bach needed money like the rest of us, but I think that even if his work was paid for, his transcriptions pay deliberate tribute to those he copied from.

Transcriptions testify to the survival value of the music, and the transcriber is a willing part of that. I don't imagine that there is a composer who has not wished to have his works perpetuated. This is one way in which that desire is accomplished.

Another thing which the transcription does is to make a work for large forces available in an area where those forces are not available. It makes the big production repeatable.

Transcription is a two way street. I heard Segovia's transcriptions of some of Bach's works years before I heard the originals. That is an example of how this can work. Hearing in one venue can take you back to another. It's strange, though, that Segovia was criticized by some at the time for bringing Bach to the guitar. He just showed us that you can bring Bach to any instrument, even those which were not in existence in Bach's day. That's what they later did with the Moog Synthesizer in "Switched-On Bach". It brought the composer to a whole new world and a whole new generation. You don't hear much about the Moog these days, although probably every synthesizer in existence is somehow related to it, but you hear more about Bach than ever.

I'm not usually one to get too excited about a remake of a classic movie, but this is a different matter. I have recordings of transcriptions such as the Canadian Brass version of the Goldberg Variations and the Emerson Quartet adaptation of The Art Of The Fugue. I also have one of a Goldberg arrangement made for string trio. I think the vitality of the music is seen in the fact that people are not content to hear it, but they want to re-create it for themselves in their own instrumental context, and others want to hear those recreations. They want to go far beneath the surface. This is almost the greatest homage that could be paid. All of these artists and composers are showing the value of Bach.

I don't know whether he would have approved or not, but others could not help but come along and follow in his footsteps and build on his life and his work in many different ways. Look at all the fugues on B - A - C - H written by various composers. Those, of course, aren't re-workings of the music, but tributes to the name. The name of Bach covered and contained his music. We know him for what he gave.

I believe that composers should get credit for what they have composed, and if anyone is going to get money for it, they should, but I think there is a larger issue involved here which is particularly proved by the work of Bach. The music itself needs to be spread as far as it can be to do the greatest possible good. If accounting stops that, then maybe we need to rethink our accounting methods.

Music is never about the ego of the composer, but about the forces unleashed in the performers and listeners. If it were just the composer, he could gloat over his scores and never even have them performed, but music is for the people who hear it.

Ultimately, the music does not belong to the composer; it belongs to God who is pleased that it grows. Composer, performer, listener are all part of the whole. That is the unifying message of Bach's ascription, S D G.

An important question that should be asked is this: What would we have had without Bach? It's hard to say, so let us ask what we have had with him. I'd say that in this one man who have more than was had before him altogether.

Bach was a door for others. Most composers tend to finish with themselves. You hear of schools of so-and-so and there are influences of such-and-such, but Bach gave a heritage which is not only pleasing to the ear, but helpful to the mind of those who would create their own great music.

By doing their transcriptions and settings of his melodies and name, those who followed were coming to a level of understanding by getting inside his methods and seeing how it was done. He helped others to mature by showing them the way.

In the long run, it would be better to allow others a free hand with what you have done than to hold on to it for yourself alone. I know from the little reading I have done in the life of Bach that he did have a struggle for financial support. He was not a multi-millionaire living off the fat of the land, but often he was more along the lines of a starving artist. Still, in the end, I believe he would have wanted his work to grow by others using it. Even if he never got paid for it, and even if those people never credited him with it, we know that in the sight of God and those who love his music, that he got to give God the glory for it.

Form confines, music liberates.

While form is valid for structuring a piece so that it can have existence, it is not in existence for its own sake. It is to be a door to the ideas of the composer, the skill of the performer and the heart of the audience.

"The Art of the Fugue" is the greatest example of any work devoted to exploring a particular form. I wouldn't say that I love it as I do Bach's other keyboard works, but I am impressed by it. Who isn't? He designed it to demonstrate what can be done with a form and to teach how it can be done by giving the player a series of pieces in which the component parts of the fugue are broken down and set forth for analysis. I don't believe another single musical form has received the treatment which the fugue received in this work. It's interesting that Bach seems to have left it almost to the last. Maybe this was something that he knew how to do so well that he didn't realize the need for others to have it broken down for them until towards the end.

Here the interest is in the musical form rather than in the keys as it had been in the Well-Tempered Clavier or in showing how to repackage a certain melody as it had been in the Goldbergs. He wants to see what can be done with this form.

I've heard this done in different mediums: piano, harpsichord, organ, and string quartet transcription. Every performing media is valid, for it adds its testimony to what is discovered when the form is explored. It shows how ideas can be adapted and transmitted in multitudinous ways. The form works wherever it is employed.

I wonder why this is called the **ART** of the fugue? Certainly, we already know that it is a musical art form. We don't have to define it as such. Bach, though, wants to prove that it is a form which can be handled and worked out to different ends at different times. He wants it to be known that music is not merely "filler" for life, but that it has a life, that it is alive. Anything which is living can react with other living things.

Bach gives us pause to think as we play or hear this work. The music itself speaks to us. Perhaps nowhere else is Bach calling us to think as much as he is in this work. I don't believe he has any particular thoughts in mind to occupy our minds, but he does want us to do something with our minds. He wants us to walk in the world.

Bach wrote in so many forms. I don't know why he chose to explore the fugue and not the toccata, fantasia, partita, rondo, polonaise or some other form to this extent and in this manner. I have to confess that I don't always know how to differentiate between them, and when I listen, I don't always care about putting the correct label on the piece I'm listening to. Unless I was attending a college class where I would be getting a grade on this material and a degree out of it, it wouldn't be necessary for me to make such a differentiation to receive from the music. It's the connection with the composer and the joy that fills when I listen that counts.

Content is above form in importance. Form is the place where the creator works out his ideas. It gives the performer a handle to express them, but they are for filling with ideas.

What did Bach give to us in these illustrations of what we ourselves should be doing?

He starts with a definite melody. Nothing is by chance. Notes don't come to a page out of the void. They always come from a person. The world of the fugue is the world of the personal. In a world in which we are told that design is false and that chance determines everything, Bach's music denies those ideas. Even modern music, which to some ears sounds more like noise than music, shouts to us of the personal. The notes don't wag the composer. They are made to go through their routine by the performer.

The idea begins it all. Thinking matters. It counts for something. It is not to be hidden under a bushel, but placed out into the world. A word which is often used in music is the word exposition. That which is inside us is exposed to the outside when it comes to music. We listen to Bach's music and know that he was orderly and interested in what was being said. He was neither haphazard or lackadaisical. Actually, we would see that in any form he chose to use, but we certainly note it here.

Then, there's harmony. That is important not only in music, but in the world as a whole. It is working with others. Even dissonance is a kind of harmony. It is notes in an off the track relationship, and it makes its own declaration of the state of affairs in the world or in the composer. I don't believe that Bach ever used dissonance, nor do I believe he would have, but had he done so, he would have been making a statement with it that he couldn't have made in any other way.

We are aware of the two handedness of the playing when we hear these. The left hand knows what the right hand is doing. Music comes out of such teamwork. The two hands work together. That's what creates the harmony. If they work independently of one another, there's no telling what it would be.

The repetition of the fugue is the fitting of the past into the present. Just because a thing occurred, doesn't mean it is finished. There's no such thing as the dead past. History is not merely important when your living it, as someone once said. What happened once echoes and resounds through the present and into the future. All choices have consequences. All consequences create effects which affect us. This means that what we do today should be carefully examined so that it will benefit us and others tomorrow and not be a burden or a horror to us.

The fugues speak in brilliance. Only players of the greatest ability can undertake these works and make them speak. Bach doesn't give us "Chopsticks", but something worthy of being played and heard until the end of time.

A door always indicates something on the other side. Sometimes, what's there is labeled. Other times, we don't know if it will be a lady or a tiger or nothing at all. There's just a door there, often locked, often unattended, but we know that it doesn't lead to a vacuum.

The music of Bach is so great that it indicates something better than it beyond it. God surely wouldn't use a talent like this to make us feel bad, that everything was going to go down hill. It's going to open on the infinite. Wherever we are at, it is going to be uphill from there.

It's not just Bach who proves this, but we are allowed to prove it as well. Our talents count for something. They are not to make us vain or to keep us laboring endlessly for the pleasure of others. They are employed to bring the best to light.

Art means that we are forever new and never old. Listen to the oldest piece of music, stand before the oldest painting, look at the oldest architecture – you are always experiencing the living. God is the God of the living, not of the dead, and what He has created in us lives.

That's why we walk through the door.

END NOTES

Music feeds us. It doesn't enter the blood stream, but it gets to the heart and goes to the head. It gives us food for thought and fuel for feeling. It nourishes us. It enriches us. It builds us up. All great music does this, and Bach's music, every kind of it, always does. When we listen we assimilate something that was not inside us before, and we grow from it.

Bach wrote for us. We are end users of his art, and yet we should not be dead end users. We are to do something with what we hear. We are to think about it, to examine it, to live it. We are to be better than we were when we have spent time with it.

Bach is not the only composer, but he gave more than any other single composer. I'm not speaking in terms of numbers or bulk of compositions, but of his heart. For years I have said that Haydn was my favorite composer. In many ways he is still a favorite, but he is not indispensable like Bach is. In the last few years I have been listening to him more than ever before.

Some things Bach did only once, but even once from his pen is enough for the ages. He proves that work can live on, that we should build with gold and silver and not with hay and stubble. The piece often proves to be greater than both the composer and the performer. I've often said of some of my own work that my songs are better than I am.

More than once I have spoken of Bach and his work as being universal. Universality covers all time and all places and all people. Bach speaks a language which can always be understood. This earth had a single language once. In heaven, we'll have it again. We'll be singing in it.

I think this may be one reason why John Eliot Gardiner used the photographs of people from around the world on the covers of his cantata series. Hardly any of those people look like people I'd find next door, at least not dressed in those costumes or sporting those hair-dos, but they are a part of the family for whom this music was written and performed. We are to get out of our boxes when we hear Bach. We are to be inclusive.

Bach speaks a language which can always be understood. He proves that we can understand one another. I don't think there is an end to what he proves. Nor should there be.

Music at its root is giving and receiving. It acts as a port of embarkation for emotions and ideas and thoughts and as a harbor to take them in. Thoughts are not negligible.

Many years ago in college I read the following lines scratched into a desk:

> Sow a thought, reap an action.
>
> Sow an action, reap a habit.
>
> Sow a habit, reap a destiny.

That's what Bach did; it's what we do, too.

14 November 2014 – 8 July 2015

13 July 2015 – 23 July 2015